MAKING A BETTER WORLD

Guardians of Wildlife

By Gary Chandler and Kevin Graham

Twenty-First Century Books

A Division of Henry Holt and Company
New York

Twenty-First Century Books
A division of Henry Holt and Company, Inc.
115 West 18th Street
New York, New York 10011

Henry Holt® and colophon are registered trademarks of
Henry Holt and Company, Inc.
Publishers since 1866

Published in Canada by Fitzhenry & Whiteside Ltd.
195 Allstate Parkway, Markham, Ontario L3R 4T8

Printed in the United States of America on acid free paper.

Created and produced in association with Blackbirch Graphics, Inc.
Series Editor: Tanya Lee Stone

Library of Congress Cataloging-in-Publication Data

Chandler, Gary.
    Guardians of wildlife / by Gary Chandler and Kevin Graham.
        p.   cm. — (Making a better world)
    Includes bibliographical references (p.   ) and index.
    Summary: Presents examples of successful efforts to protect wildlife and
includes the names and addresses of organizations involved in these endeavors.
    ISBN 0-8050-4626-7
    1. Wildlife conservation—Juvenile literature. 2. Wildlife management—Juvenile
literature. [1. Wildlife conservation. 2. Wildlife management.] I. Graham, Kevin
II. Title. III. Series: Making a better world (New York, N.Y.)
QL83.C47   1996
639.9—dc20
                                                                                96-2912
                                                                                  CIP
                                                                                   AC

Table of Contents

In your lifetime, several species of animals will vanish from the face of the earth forever. In fact, it has already happened. The question is how many more losses will occur, and what they will mean to the earth and its people.

At one time, wild animals and wide-open spaces outnumbered humans on this planet. But over time, the balance shifted—taking a toll on species such as tigers, elephants, gorillas, and countless others. Fortunately, governments, conservation organizations, and individuals around the world are trying to intervene. Environmental problems tackled by conservationists have begun to help specific threatened and endangered species—some problems have been solved while others still persist. Today, modern conservation efforts take a broad look at species protection. Part of the focus has shifted to entire ecosystems and the wildlife habitat they provide. For example, saving forest areas will result in saving the animal and plant species living there.

Illegal hunters, or poachers, pose another serious threat to many animals. The rhinoceros, for instance, has been hunted to the brink of extinction in Africa because people can sell its horns illegally for a lot of money. Poachers will shoot an animal, cut off its horn, and leave the remains to the scavengers of the wild, depleting the species.

In other cases, species have been threatened by human-made poisons and toxins. The bald eagle and the peregrine falcon nearly became extinct because of a poison called DDT. It was used by farmers as an insecticide and it contaminated many food and water supplies. As a result, eagles, falcons, and other animals absorbed so much of the poison that many died. Even the eagles and falcons that survived, however, were afflicted with a problem that killed most of their young: Their egg shells were often too weak and thin to survive the mother's weight during incubation (keeping the egg warm as the embryo inside develops).

Fortunately, the use of DDT has been stopped in the United States and several other countries. Unfortunately, it is still widely used around the world.

All of the books in *Making a Better World* report on people—kids, parents, schools, neighborhoods, and companies—who have decided to get involved in a cause they believe in. Through their dedication, commitment, and dreams, they helped to make ours a better world. Each of the stories in this book will take you through the steps of what it took for some ordinary people to achieve something extraordinary. Of course, in the space of one book, we can share only a fraction of the wonderful stories that exist. After a long and complicated selection process, we have chosen what we believe are the most exciting subjects to tell you about.

We hope this book will encourage you to learn more about the issues of endangered species, habitat conservation, and bio-diversity. Better yet, we hope all the books in this series inspire you to get involved. There are plenty of ways that each individual—including you—can make a better world. You will find some opportunities throughout this book—and there are many others out there waiting for you to discover. If you would like to write to us for more information, the address is Earth News, P.O. Box 101413, Denver, CO 80250.

Sincerely,

Gary Chandler
and
Kevin Graham

Tracking the Animals
of the World

*S*pecies of plants and animals are be-
coming extinct at a rapid rate. The information lost with
them is impossible to imagine, therefore studies and conservation efforts are extremely important. Fortunately, there have
been several efforts launched to help take inventory of, or
track, various threatened species around the world. Also, in
Vietnam, Russia, and China, discoveries of previously unknown
animal species have been made in recent years. These efforts
have helped conservationists in their fight to save the habitats
necessary for the long-term survival of countless animal species.

Photo-Trapping Leads to
Rhino Repopulation

Indonesia has some of the most diverse wildlife and plant species in the world. It also has the fourth-largest human population in the world. These combined factors present a major conservation challenge to this island nation just north of Australia. One of the most endangered of all Indonesian mammals is the Javan rhinoceros, named for Java, a western island in Indonesia.

Despite their huge size, Javan rhinos move quickly and quietly through tangles of vines and thick walls of shrubs. By dropping their heads, the animals move like huge wedges that push the undergrowth up and over their backs as they plow through the vegetation. Trapping one of these rare and rugged rhinos for scientific studies and census (population count) work is no easy task. Fortunately for the international scientists and local Indonesians studying the animal, a new form of trapping has been used at Ujung Kulon National Park on Java.

No nets, fences, tranquilizers, or helicopters (methods commonly used by researchers) were used to round up and subdue the animals for intensive observation. Instead, cameras were used to "trap" rhinos on film in their native domain. This effort marked the first time photo-trapping technology had been used to conduct a full-fledged census of an endangered species. Now that this photo technique has been successful, it can be applied to count other endangered species around the world.

"The technology had been used before to photograph scenic shots of wildlife, but in this instance, we were pushing the technology in a new direction to tell us how many animals were left in existence—in essence we pioneered the operation on this scale," says Mike Griffith. He is the leader of the joint effort between the World Wildlife Fund and the Indonesian government to count the rhinos and make recommendations on how to save them from extinction.

As late as the 1880s, thousands of rhinos wandered all over the island of Java. Then the Dutch government—which had colonized the island 100 years earlier—decided to put a bounty on the rhinos because they were seen as pests. Just 40 years later, the rhino faced extinction. Only a handful had survived and lived in a small wild area at the southwestern tip of the island. The Dutch then created a wildlife reserve in 1921 to give the remaining animals a chance to survive. Thus Ujung

Mike Griffith points out the location of Ujung Kulon National Park.

Kulon National Park was created, although it didn't officially become a national park until 60 years later in 1981. The park now is one of the few undeveloped areas on the most heavily populated island in the world.

By the 1970s, the rhinos' numbers had finally climbed to an estimated 70 or 80 animals. Then, in 1981, a mysterious disease swept through the small population, killing an unknown number. "Five carcasses were found, but my guess is that many more died during that time," Griffith reports. Since then, no one has had a clear idea of how many rhinos still existed in the park. That is why, in 1990, Griffith set out on a two-year mission to count the remaining animals.

Mike Griffith developed his photo-trapping skills while working on a photography book that featured the various wildlife of Sumatra, the large Indonesian island northwest of Java. Over time, the secrets he learned made his photo-trapping work as flawless as possible. But before making the big jump from photographer to conservationist, and launching into the photo-trapping project, Griffith knew that he needed to recruit a team of local people to help him conduct the census. The superintendent of Ujung Kulon picked two of his park rangers to join Griffith in the effort. The rangers then visited nearby villages until five more men were found who were willing to go on extended expeditions into the forest. "This team became one of the most satisfying parts of the whole experience," Griffith says. "They showed a lot of courage, humor and a great work ethic. In the end we were a happy, dedicated team of jungle folk."

Griffith systematically set up cameras along well-used rhino trails since catching rhinos out in the brush was difficult. Often, machetes (swordlike knives) had to be used to cut through the thick vegetation in order to reach the camera locations. Each camera was set to be triggered by a pressure-sensitive mat that was laid on the ground, barely buried under an animal trail. When an animal stepped on the mat, its weight would trip the camera's trigger.

9

Griffith and his team set out to check all of their camera locations.

After each camera was set up, the first shot on every roll of film was taken of a team member standing on the photo mat. Their weight would activate a picture of a member holding a survey pole and a sign showing the name of the location. The survey pole provided a simple way to accurately measure the height of whatever walked by from that point on.

As all kinds of animals walked down the paths, pictures were taken of them. Film was collected every four or five weeks. In all, 576 rolls of film were shot during the census—a total of more than 20,000 pictures of various Indonesian wildlife moving through the forest. Each shot showed a date and time of exposure, so the scientists could tell if a leopard was on the heels of a pig, for example. "In the end, we got a breakdown of all the animals of Java," Griffith notes. "We had a lot of pictures of wild boars, along with shots of wild buffalo, three types of deer, otters, both black and spotted leopards, and wild dogs. Even a peacock triggered a camera one time."

And, thankfully, Javan rhinos also were captured on film. Several times close-up shots showed the animals' faces—with huge flared nostrils—as they came near to sniff the camera equipment and trigger yet another photo. A crucial part of the study involved identifying individual rhinos so a realistic count could be made. Griffith painstakingly accomplished this by spending hours with a magnifying glass, viewing slide after slide. A series of different observations allowed him to mark individual animals. He studied heights, horn shapes, unique scars, and even skin pores. "After noting the date and time of day when the rhino passed the camera, the most important thing was to identify the individual," he explains. "All future population calculations based on the field data depended on identifying individual rhinos."

Over the course of the census project, some of the rhinos ended up being caught on film more than a dozen times each

This Javan rhino was "trapped" by Griffith's technology.

in different camera locations. This good fortune gave Griffith an idea of what these animals' home ranges are. One animal's territory measured at least 6 miles long and 4 miles wide. In the end, the photo-trapping effort and subsequent calculation revealed a Javan rhino population of about 46 animals in Ujung Kulon National Park. Along with about a dozen similar animals in the country of Vietnam, this count was crucial in showing that the total population of Javan rhinos remains dangerously low. Now everyone knows roughly how many animals remain. This has increased overall awareness and concern is up.

In a presentation to the Indonesian government, Griffith stressed the importance of security measures in Ujung Kulon to ensure that no poaching will take place in the future. Even though poaching has not been a recent problem with the one-horned rhino, he feels the limited population must be aggressively protected. Rhino populations in other parts of the world have been hunted for their horns. In those cases, the horns have been sold illegally for use in Asian medicines. Griffith stressed that this threat must be kept away from the remaining Javan rhinos. In the end, Griffith was able to successfully introduce a humane technique for counting a small animal population, which will directly help to revitalize the species.

The International Union for Conservation of Nature has proposed an ultimate goal of raising the Javan rhino population to 2,000 animals. It's a difficult goal, but one Griffith hopes is eventually reached. "I developed a real kinship with the rhinos during this work, and I'm absolutely committed to them," he exclaims. "I hope this effort makes sure these rhinos get a chance to survive. And hopefully, it will lead to other conservation efforts, as well."

For More Information

Write to the World Wildlife Fund Indonesia Program, P.O. Box 7928, Jakarta, Indonesia 12079.

Saving Birds of Prey

Another successful conservation story involves the peregrine falcon. When this creature reached the verge of extinction, The Peregrine Fund sprang to life. Since then, the nonprofit group has revived the peregrine species and now works to save many other birds of prey.

Tom Cade, a professor, started the organization at Cornell University in 1970. At the time, the peregrine falcon had already vanished east of the Mississippi River, and 80 to 90 percent of the population had vanished in the West. However, thanks to the banning of the pesticide DDT and The Peregrine Fund's captive breeding and reintroduction program, the peregrine falcon is now making a strong recovery. "In cooperation with other organizations, we've already released 4,000 peregrines in 28 states," says Bill Burnham, president and CEO of The Peregrine Fund. In 1975, there were only 39 known pairs of falcons in the United States. As of 1995, about 1,300 pairs of falcons were living in the continental United States, with about 90 of those pairs living in cities. About a dozen pairs live in New York City, where they prey on the local pigeon population. In 1995, the U.S. Fish and Wildlife Service was able to take initial steps to remove the peregrine falcon from the Endangered Species List, where it has been included since 1970.

A peregrine falcon and its young were photographed high on a Baltimore, Maryland, building.

California condors such as this from the Los Angeles Zoo, have been used in The Peregrine Fund's condor breeding program.

Due to The Peregrine Fund's success with the peregrine falcon, the group has since been asked to participate on projects in more than 35 countries. To date, it has hatched and raised birds from 22 different raptor (birds of prey) species. In 1992, at the request of the California Condor Recovery Team, the U.S. Fish and Wildlife Service selected The Peregrine Fund to operate the world's third California condor breeding program. A 17,000 square-foot condor facility was built in 1993 at The Peregrine Fund's headquarters near Boise, Idaho. Six pairs of condors were sent there from the Los Angeles Zoo and the San Diego Wild Animal Park. Four additional pairs arrived in November 1994.

The U.S. Fish and Wildlife Service has released a total of 27 condors into the wild. Unfortunately, 4 of them died from hitting power lines and 1 died from eating antifreeze. Nine of the other released condors were recaptured and brought back to the breeding facility for re-release into a more remote area. In June 1996, The Peregrine Fund released condors near the Grand Canyon.

Raptors are good indicator-species for the overall health of the environment. An indicator species is one that is high enough on the food chain—the order in which organisms feed on one another in an ecosystem—to be quickly affected by an unhealthy ecosystem. When these species become threatened, it is likely as a result of a greater environmental problem. For example, the pesticide DDT was outlawed in part because of its destructive effect on eagle, falcon, and other bird populations.

One of The Peregrine Fund's most dramatic discoveries occurred in Madagascar, a large island off the eastern coast of Africa. In the 1930's, the last Madagascar serpent-eagle and last Madagascar red owl were reportedly shot and stuffed for a museum in Paris. However, on November 2, 1993, Peregrine Fund biologists made the first serpent-eagle sighting in more than 60 years. They later trapped one of the birds, banded it for later identification, and released it for study in the wild.

In October 1994, Peregrine Fund biologists found, trapped, and tagged a Madagascar red owl. Information about these species is being used to promote additional conservation activities in Africa and Madagascar.

Martin Baba gets ready to release a Madagascar red owl during a Peregrine Fund project.

Partly as a result of the discovery of these species, the largest single block of lowland rainforest left in Madagascar will be formally designated a national park. The Masoala

National Park will protect 810 square miles of pristine wilderness and rare habitat. The new park will become the largest protected area in Madagascar, an island known for its unique biological diversity and one of the world's top conservation priorities. "The rediscovery of the Madagascar serpent-eagle helped justify the creation of the park," says Rick Watson, program director for The Peregrine Fund's Africa programs. The general plan to set up the Masoala National Park was approved by the Madagascar Department of Water and Forests in February 1995.

The Peregrine Fund is also working to save tropical forests in Central America, where the Fund's "Maya Project" is located at the Maya ruins of Tikal in Guatemala. Here a large area was recently declared a "Biosphere Reserve." The Maya Project involves field studies on birds of prey, resident and migrant songbirds, and forest vegetation, providing managers of the Biosphere Reserve with information that can help conserve the forest.

Most field work is done by local people, who learn by working along with university students such as Russell Thorstrom. He studied raptors at Tikal while earning a master's degree. Two local brothers, Julio and Hector Madrid, have become experts on the ornate hawk-eagle, a handsome crested species. They have documented the species' diet and nesting success, and, by tracking radio-tagged birds, have demonstrated the amount of forest habitat the birds require. Based on this work, The Peregrine Fund estimates that Tikal National Park's 222 square miles (576 square kilometers) are home to about 85 pairs of ornate hawk-eagles. This information helps determine whether the park can maintain a healthy population of hawk-eagles if surrounding areas become deforested. Similar studies are underway or complete on some 17 raptor species.

The main threat to Central American forests is expansion of cattle ranching and slash-and-burn farming. Says David Whitacre, the project director, "Farmers typically cut down a few acres of forest, then burn it, releasing nutrients into the soil. Then they plant corn with a digging stick among the ashes. After one or two crops, the soil loses fertility while weeds and insect pests increase, so the farmer cuts another patch of forest for the next year's crop. It's a good system when only a few farmers are using it, but today there are too many farmers chipping away at the vanishing forest."

Because of this, The Peregrine Fund hired Chindo Garcia, a local farmer, to introduce farmers from his village to a method that consumes less forest. Chindo has provided 121 local farmers with seed of *"Frijol de Abono"* or "fertilizer bean." Like other members of the pea family, this plant has bacteria on its roots that convert nitrogen from the air into a form usable by plants. This increases corn yields and allows farmers to repeatedly farm the same acreage instead of cutting down more forest each year. It also chokes out weeds, decreasing the need for back-breaking labor. These farmers have now established *Frijol de Abono* plantations equal in area to 138 football fields! Soon they will plant corn here. Hopefully, increased corn yields will convince them to permanently adopt this method, which should slow deforestation. As Chindo says, "This is the best of both worlds—the farmers make a better living with less work, and Julio and Hector's ornate hawk-eagles will still have a home."

A Peregrine Fund worker from the Maya Project, Rudolfo Cruz, climbs a tall tree to study a hawk-eagle.

For More Information

Write to The Peregrine Fund, World Center for Birds of Prey, 5666 W. Flying Hawk Lane, Boise, ID 83709, or call (208) 362-8687. You can also find them on the World Wide Web at http://www.peregrinefund.org

World's Largest Animal Database

In a different type of effort, one group is compiling and organizing volumes of data on the world's many threatened and endangered species.

Until recently, many biologists were forced to spend valuable research time in libraries looking for data on species that often was incomplete or inaccurate. Now, field biologists can rely on the Threatened and Endangered Species Information Institute (TESII) for basic information, while spending more time in the field conducting investigations and gathering new information on rare species. The Colorado-based, nonprofit organization is creating the world's largest library on threatened and endangered species with the goal of providing the information to anyone who wants to learn more about these animals and the issues surrounding them.

TESII was created by a group of biologists and concerned environmentalists. The group knew the frustrations of searching for reliable information, and they recognized the need for centralized species information. All information the institute obtains is evaluated and verified by qualified biologists to ensure accuracy. Many other sources of information, including the Endangered Species Technical Bulletins produced by the U.S. Fish and Wildlife Service, have also been added to the library.

Recovery plans, soil surveys, hydrology (water) maps, and wetlands maps are just a few examples of materials available through TESII. In the process of building the library, the

institute also came across highly classified species information. This is made available only to scientists that genuinely need the information. "We do have specific habitat locations that are not available to the general public," explains Iris Kendall, executive director of TESII. "Unfortunately there are people that would go out and catch the last desert tortoise if they knew exactly where the remaining population existed."

The majority of the information at TESII, however, is not restricted. The institute creates teaching packets for schools, as well as interactive exhibits for local school tours. The group also hopes to build a museum in 1997. "We're also producing two CD-ROM packages for wildlife professionals and educators," Kendall notes. "One of our long-range goals is to have our records on-line so they can be accessed by personal computers all over the world. If people will just learn and understand our natural environment, we can minimize our negative impacts."

The black-footed ferret (left) and the jaguarundi (right) are just two of the endangered animals that TESII has included in their library of information.

For More Information

Write to the Threatened and Endangered Species Information Institute, 18301 West Colfax Avenue, Building R104, Golden, CO 80401, or call (303) 278-0956.

Saving Threatened and Endangered Species

Growing human populations around the world, and our demand for natural resources such as wood, water, land, and fossil fuels, have destroyed the habitat necessary for many animals to survive. These actions have also altered the delicate balance of nature, creating some effects that we may not even be aware of. By understanding the needs of animals, humans can allow them to live more undisturbed lives. A deeper understanding can also help humans better handle conservation efforts that are most vital to the survival of certain species.

Many animal preservation efforts take place in the wild—in an animal's natural habitat. Others are aimed at education and operate in zoos. Sometimes it is beneficial to study a few animals in captivity and educate people who would otherwise not have a chance to observe, and therefore learn, about an animal. Both types of study will be explored in this chapter.

The Wild Dolphin Project

There are plant and animal species that have already become extinct and some that are reaching the point of extinction. For humans, knowledge about animals that are extinct has already been lost. In an effort to learn about some species of dolphins before we have lost the chance, a unique research effort is taking place in their natural habitat—the ocean. This information will add to the research already conducted on these animals in captivity. Called the Wild Dolphin Project, the effort began in 1985 and looks at the life history and communication systems of a resident group of Atlantic spotted dolphins in the Bahamas. "By letting researchers observe them in their natural world and on their terms, these dolphins allow us to learn things about their social structure, communication system, habitat and many other aspects of their lives that have never before been studied in the wild," says Dr. Denise Herzing, the project's research director.

The project, which will run until the year 2004, gathers data, analyzes and interprets it, and then communicates the results to both the scientific community and the general public. It is designed to study the animals in and around a shallow sandbank in the Atlantic Ocean. The exceptionally clear water and the continuous presence of the dolphins in the area allow for extended periods of underwater observation. Still cameras are used to photograph the dolphins' natural world, and video cameras are used to record their movements and sounds.

The project's leaders believe that the best way to learn about dolphin behavior is to observe the animals in their own habitat. While similar work has been done with gorillas and chimpanzees, this is the only such work involving dolphins. The long length of the study allows researchers to document the life history of the dolphins in a natural setting. In addition to gathering scientific research, the project also educates people about the dolphins and the need to protect their habitat.

Although the Atlantic spotted dolphin is not on the list of threatened animals, severe pollution is threatening all ocean life. "As top-feeding predators, dolphins and whales are vulnerable to certain types of pollution—primarily chemicals that can't be seen. It's the invisible threat," Herzing reports. "They store it [chemicals] in their fat and mothers pass it on to their babies through their milk. Ocean pollution is the number one threat to the Atlantic spotted dolphin and many other species." One of the greatest challenges facing the study involved learning when and how to work with the animals without intruding on the dolphins' lives. "They all have different personalities—some are shy, some exploratory, some make better mothers than others—they're all different," notes Herzing.

The Wild Dolphin Project has been able to gather an enormous amount of information on these dolphins. The spotted dolphin is usually found in groups of up to 50 animals, although larger groups do exist.

Dr. Denise Herzing swims with a spotted dolphin and her underwater camera.

A typical adult is about 6 feet long and weighs roughly 200 pounds. The female dolphins are slightly larger than the males. Individual spotted dolphins can be identified over time by their spot patterns, and nicks and notches in their dorsal fins and flukes (tail flippers). Dolphins also have whistles that are as unique as each human voice. Pregnancy for an Atlantic spotted dolphin lasts 11 months, and a baby calf can nurse for up to 5 years. Baby dolphins are dark gray with white undersides and have no spots. As the animals mature, both white and dark spots emerge to form unique patterns. They reach maturity after about 12-to-15 years. Juvenile spotted dolphins are known to "babysit" the younger offspring in their groups.

A gang of mothers and infants glides by underwater photographers from the Wild Dolphin Project.

The Atlantic spotted dolphin is found all the way from South America to Europe—in both tropical and temperate waters. Herzing reports that, "The greatest accomplishment so far has been tracking individual animals for ten years and being able to understand their communication system—its development and complexity."

The Wild Dolphin Project, through the information and images collected since 1985, has greatly influenced many decisions made by the tuna industry to stop using dolphin-killing fishing techniques. The Wild Dolphin Project plans on continuing to make a big impact in the fight to protect the ocean's inhabitants from threats to their survival.

For More Information
Write to the Wild Dolphin Project, P.O. Box 3839, Palos Verdes, CA 90274, or call (310) 791-5878.

Every Which Way But Loose

In Southeast Asia, the countries of Indonesia and Malaysia are the focal points of a desperate struggle for survival. This struggle was not helped when Clint Eastwood appeared in a movie with a pet orangutan. After the movie came out, thousands of these animals were taken from their native jungles. The movie title, *Every Which Way But Loose*, now describes the plight of the endangered orangutan species.

The wildlife markets in Taiwan—which are an unregulated combination of outdoor markets, storefronts, and individual street peddlers—are not able to keep up with people's requests for baby orangutans. Hundreds, and possibly thousands, of the baby primates have been smuggled out of the jungles of Sumatra and Borneo and sold as pets. Smugglers shoot and kill the mother orangutans in order to take their babies. "It's hard to say how many orangutans have died due to the wildlife trade, but we've heard of thousands of them actually making it to Taiwan," says Willie Smits, an expert on the species in East Kalimantan, Indonesia.

After Smits rescued a baby orangutan from a wildlife market in Balikpapan, East Kalimantan, he started a remarkable program that could save hundreds of these endangered animals. With the help of several schoolchildren, the Balikpapan Orangutan Society, and the Indonesian government, an orangutan "reintroduction center" was established at the Wanariset Station. A medical clinic, a quarantine area (holding area to prevent the spread of disease), and several large cages were built. More than 80 baby orangutans have already been brought to the center to begin their journey back to the jungle. "We

successfully returned 28 orangutans to the rainforest in the first 18 months of the program," Smits reported in 1993. As of March 1996, the center had returned more than 50.

"Once there were millions of orangutans living throughout Asia. Now there are only about 20,000 left in the wild," Smits adds. Habitat destruction, poaching, and smuggling have all taken their toll on this red-haired ape. Today, these animals are only found in their natural habitats on two islands in the entire world—Borneo and Sumatra. Thanks to Smits, a more aggressive protection program is now in effect in Indonesia— the country that governs all of Sumatra and most of Borneo. As Smits explains, "The first thing that we needed was a facility that could properly care for confiscated animals. A baby orangutan typically spends about five years with its mother before it is ready to live on its own. Therefore, a confiscated animal

Schoolchildren from Pasir Ridge International School in Balikpapan helped raise funds for the reintroduction center.

Willie Smits checks in on an orangutan at Wanariset.

has no chance to survive alone in the jungle without a support group and adequate preparation."

Officially, orangutans have been protected by Indonesian law since 1925, but confiscating an illegally kept orangutan has been a very complicated process. In the past, whenever a government official found someone in possession of an orangutan, the animal either had to be released immediately or put to sleep. Since the government rarely had the facilities or the training to properly prepare the apes for release and officials did not want to destroy the animals, few orangutans were ever confiscated. Thanks to the new center, the Indonesian government has started to crack down on smugglers.

When an orangutan arrives at Wanariset Station, it spends at least two to three weeks in quarantine and receives medical treatment. Once an animal is released from quarantine, it is placed in a cage with another orangutan of similar size. Since these animals are babies that have left their adult role models, the new arrivals learn how to interact from their roommates.

After an adjustment period, both are moved to a compartment near a large, outdoor, socialization cage where, from a safe distance, they can observe even more animals of their own species for possibly the very first time. Both groups smell, touch, and watch each other through the bars. "After the newness wears off, we open the doors and let them interact with each other. We watch them closely to avoid fighting. But they all quickly learn their role in the group," Smits says.

Since these animals were taken from the jungle when they were quite young, the reintroduction center must help them learn many basic survival skills. About 100 specific food items are taken from the area where the animals will eventually be released so that they will be familiar with what food they need to eat.

Other programs in Southeast Asia have helped orphaned orangutans, but the center that Smits has created is unique in many ways. Most notably, the animals at Wanariset have minimal human contact and few visitors are allowed. In the other "rehabilitation" centers, many visitors are welcome to play with the orangutans, which makes it harder for them to successfully return to the wild.

Another difference is how and where the animals are released. Other centers, for example, take a single animal out and release it near the rehabilitation center. Often, the animal will find its way back to the center for an easy meal and even bring wild orangutans back with them. Instead of enabling the rehabilitated animals to return to their natural habitat, the wild orangutans begin to act like tame animals.

In addition, other programs have offered minimal medical assistance and run the risk of releasing sick or infected animals. The practice can infect an entire population, killing even more of these endangered animals.

At the Wanariset Station, the reintroduction team has addressed these problems. The animals are released as a group. Typically, about 15 to 20 orangutans are turned loose together so they can continue learning from each other as they

An orangutan named Dodoy was one of the center's first animals to be reintroduced to the wild.

explore their new home. They also depend on each other for security during this critical introductory phase. Orangutans are not solitary animals. Adults will typically give each other territorial space, but mothers intentionally bring their young together to play.

The animals from the Wanariset Station are released in the protected Sungai Wain forest area, in East Kalimantan—an area that does not have an existing orangutan population. The apes are moved out to the forest and placed in a wooden cage that will decompose on its own within a few days. This gives the orangutans a chance to get used to their new home in a secure environment.

The reintroduction program was initially proposed in 1970 by one of Smits's colleagues, Dr. Herman Rijksen, a Dutch primatologist working on the Indonesian island of Sumatra. The Indonesian Office of the World Wildlife Fund also endorsed this approach in 1990. To date, however, the Wanariset Station is the only center actually using this approach. The first group of orangutans was released from Wanariset on May 23, 1992. Another group was released on February 1, 1993, and a third group was released in the summer of 1993.

After the animals are returned to the wild, the second phase of the program begins and the reintroduction team tracks them from a distance. The animals are observed and their activities are recorded.

As with many species, the biggest long-term threat to the survival of the orangutan is habitat destruction. The slash-and-burn farming that is practiced by nomadic farmers destroys prime orangutan habitat. After just a few years, this land is unsuitable for most vegetation and wildlife. Locating and teaching all of these nomadic farmers to rely on more sustainable production techniques will be a long and slow process, but the effort has begun. Logging has also taken its toll on the orangutans' habitat, but some loggers are now using selective-harvesting techniques in these areas to reduce the impact caused by this industry. Selective harvesting allows loggers to remove only a certain number of trees per acre instead of clearing an entire area.

The orangutan, however, still has a tough battle ahead. "If you look at what percentage of the remaining orangutans live in protected areas, you'll find that it's only about 6 percent. They are very, very threatened. With only about 20,000 of these animals left in the world—that's the equivalent of a small village. It won't take much to make that village disappear," Smits laments.

For More Information

Write to the Balikpapan Orangutan Society, c/o Wanariset I Samboja, P.O. Box 319, Balikpapan, Indonesia 76013.

Save the Tiger Fund

A conservation challenge is occurring in Asia—the fight for the majestic tiger. Three subspecies of tigers have already been pushed into extinction in the last 50 years. If conditions don't change, the remaining wild tigers will have only a few more years on our planet. A new American-based program hopes to curb this deadly trend.

The National Fish and Wildlife Foundation (NFWF) and the Exxon Corporation formed the Save the Tiger Fund in September 1995. It is a broad-based conservation program aimed at assisting the long-term survival of the five remaining subspecies of tigers. All five of the subspecies are endangered. Amos Eno, executive director of NFWF, says, "The Save the Tiger Fund will be the most comprehensive and in-depth tiger

Amos Eno launched the Save the Tiger Fund program in September 1995.

conservation program ever conducted. It will coordinate international conservation activities, scientific research and public education to help save tigers."

This effort is supervised by an independent council consisting of several leading zoologists, conservationists, and tiger authorities. It is managed by NFWF, an organization that has handled 48 conservation funds and supported more than 1,200 conservation projects around the world. The Save the Tiger Fund's goals are to help stabilize and improve tiger populations in the wild; to promote habitat protection throughout Asia—the only region of the world where tigers are found; to enhance conservation breeding programs at zoos in the United States, Europe, Asia, and Australia; and to educate the public about the need for tiger conservation.

"The number of wild tigers has fallen an estimated 95 percent this century alone, to what the World Conservation Union estimated was 4,600 to 7,400 remaining animals," Eno says. In the last 50 years, the Caspian, Javan, and Bali tigers have become extinct and there are less than 80 South China tigers left in the wild. The greatest threats to tigers are poaching and habitat destruction by people. Tiger bones and body parts are sold on the black market for use in traditional Chinese medicines, and the forests where they live are being destroyed for timber and farming.

By 1996, the fund had provided $1 million in grants for ten different projects. To help protect the remaining 300 to 400 Siberian tigers, the fund sponsored a field research program in the Sikhote-Alin preserve in eastern Russia. Through this program, tigers are captured, fitted with radio collars, and tracked throughout their range. The project also educates the public on general forest ecology so people can learn to care for their environment. In addition, about 260 square miles of forest next to the Sikhote-Alin preserve have been purchased, which increases the protected range of the Siberian tiger.

In Indonesia, it is estimated that there are fewer than 500 Sumatran tigers left in the wild. The Save the Tiger Fund has

A Siberian tiger is fitted with a radio collar for research purposes.

supported a research project on the island of Sumatra similar to the one in the Sikhote-Alin preserve because of this low estimate. In addition to using radio collars, photo-traps are hidden in the jungle to photograph any animal that steps on triggers placed along game trails. (This photo-trapping technology was inspired by the Javan rhino study discussed in Chapter 1.) Antipoaching efforts are also a key part of the Sumatran effort to protect the remaining tigers.

In addition to these projects, the Save the Tiger Fund also sponsors efforts to help the Indochinese tigers of China, Laos, Malaysia, and Thailand. The fund is also responsible for programs that breed tigers in captivity in Moscow, Russia, and Tokyo, Japan, as well as public education campaigns with the Smithsonian Institution and the National Zoological Park in Washington, D.C.

For More Information

Write to the Save the Tiger Fund, National Fish and Wildlife Foundation, 1120 Connecticut Avenue, NW, Suite 900, Washington, DC, 20036. You can also call 1-800-5TIGERS and learn all about tigers and conservation efforts through their voice mail menu. Or see the World Wide Web for their home page at http://www.5tigers.org

Preserving Habitats
for Wildlife

*U*nderstanding the needs of various species is an important step toward conservation of all animals. However, acting on this knowledge and working to preserve animal habitat is the ultimate goal of this process. Animal habitat is often thought of as just rainforests, old-growth forests, wetlands, and oceans. In reality, animal habitat is found almost everywhere, including your backyard, city park, nearby fields, and local streams and rivers. You can get involved at almost any level—locally or internationally. You can support wildlife conservation in many ways, including volunteerism, memberships, donations, and supporting companies that donate a portion of their profits to wildlife conservation. You can also build bird nests in your neighborhood, or convince your parents to stop using pesticides on your lawn. All of these efforts can make a difference.

Incentives to Save Lives

The African Wildlife Foundation believes that there is a strong connection between the health and welfare of people and the ultimate survival and support of the animals of a region. To this end, the Foundation has developed many programs in Africa that will provide a better future for the continent's wildlife and its varied ecosystems as well as benefit the local people. One program, called Neighbors As Partners, was originally developed with the Tanzania National Parks and returns a portion of the money earned by the national parks to local communities through an innovative program of aid to community-initiated projects. The money is used for new schoolrooms, health care clinics, water wells, and other projects that improve life for people. "If you can make the parks work for the people—the people will work for the parks," says R. Michael Wright, president of the African Wildlife Foundation. "By allowing local people to benefit from wildlife, they will end up helping protect the wildlife from poaching and will share their land with animals." Neighbors As Partners works directly with communities surrounding various parks to get the people involved and committed to the well-being of the animals there.

Started in 1961 by Russell Train—who also founded the World Wildlife Fund—the African Wildlife Foundation has 35 other ongoing projects in Africa. The Foundation is head-quartered in Washington, D.C., but maintains most of its staff in field offices in Kenya, Tanzania, Rwanda, Uganda, and Zaire. Its goal is to help African people and their institutions become stronger and more independent in the struggle to save Africa's natural resources.

The foundation helped establish Tanzania's College of African Wildlife Management at Mweke—the first English-speaking institution in Africa where native Africans are trained in natural resource management. The group also supports workshops for rangers and wardens who work at wildlife parks and reserves in Africa.

In addition, the foundation conducts programs to help protect specific endangered animals that are native to Africa, such as elephants, rhinos, and mountain gorillas. Activities include the longest-running study of elephants, support for the protection and re-introduction of black rhinos in Tsavo National Park, and the development of gorilla-based ecotourism and community development in Uganda. "Our work involves education and training. By protecting the wildlife, we hope to help the local people benefit from the animals," Wright says. "Our ultimate goal is for African institutions and people to take care of the wildlife. In the end, we'd like to put ourselves out of a job."

Norah Njiraini studies elephants at the Amboseli Elephant Research Program in Kenya.

For More Information

Send a self-addressed stamped envelope to the African Wildlife Foundation, 1717 Massachusetts Avenue NW, Washington, D.C. 20036.

Corporate Lands Become Wildlife Habitat

In America, another organization has preserved habitat by showing corporations how an investment in wildlife can actually lower maintenance costs on their property. The Wildlife Habitat Council, formed in 1988, helps large landholders, especially corporations, manage their unused lands for the benefit of wildlife.

There is a limited amount of public land that is designated for the protection of wildlife in the United States. That amount will probably not increase very much as more and more land is used for development. But private corporations own large areas of land that remain undeveloped. The council's goal is to convince these landowners that it would not only be beneficial to the environment, but profitable for them to invest their property in wildlife habitat. For example, DuPont Company's Kinston, North Carolina, fiber manufacturing plant has saved $267 per acre in grounds maintenance costs since 1991 when it began a meadow restoration project on 200 acres. The project provides a home and feeding grounds for a variety of birds and white-tailed deer, while reducing costs for the company. "We use wildlife as a vehicle to build trust and communication between companies and communities," says Joyce Kelly, president of the Wildlife Habitat Council. "Wildlife can help people find common ground."

The council teaches industry and business how to support wildlife and encourages the public to learn more about wildlife by participating in voluntary habitat projects. Volunteer wildlife

teams from communities work together to maintain ongoing habitat programs, including planting trees, building nest boxes, constructing nature trails, and providing raptor perches. The council works primarily with corporate landholders. It has more than 100 corporate members, including Ford, DuPont, and U.S. Steel. The group also works with ski areas like Winter Park, Mt. Bachelor, and Aspen to provide wildlife information and educational displays at ski resorts where people and wildlife often come in contact with each other.

The council's projects now cover more than 310,000 acres at 347 sites in six countries. All private lands—from industrial city sites to rural settings—offer opportunities for wildlife. In Waterloo, Iowa, Deere & Company's engine works facility restored a native prairie and reduced its ground maintenance

Children from a local school visit a preserved wetland at U.S. Steel.

Nesting boxes are installed on a quarry site that has been protected with the help of the Wildlife Habitat Council.

costs by $638 per acre because the land didn't require mowing, watering, fertilizing, or weeding. General Electric restored a meadow in Schenectady, New York, and now saves about $530 per acre every year on maintenance costs.

"Ecological land management practices often result in significant cost savings over traditional methods," Kelly explains. "And companies are finding that wildlife programs also are good for employee morale and community relations."

For More Information
Write to the Wildlife Habitat Council, 1010 Wayne Street, Suite 920, Silver Spring, MD 20910, or call (301) 588-8994.

The Florida Panthers Defend Their Namesake

One professional hockey team is getting in the game—the players are fighting for the endangered Florida panther. It all started when a National Hockey League (NHL) team from Florida asked the public for help in selecting a name for its new sports organization.

"After just a few weeks, it became clear the overwhelming choice was Florida Panthers," says team spokesman Greg Bouris. The hockey team then decided to create the Panther Saves program in cooperation with Save the Panther, Inc., a nonprofit conservation organization run by the National Fish and Wildlife Foundation (NFWF) dedicated to helping the Florida panther. "If we were going to take the name, the team's owner felt it would be irresponsible if we didn't try to help this animal," Bouris adds.

The Florida panther is the state animal and is considered one of the most endangered mammals on earth. In 1982, following a poll of elementary students, the Florida legislature declared the panther the state animal. The Florida panther is one of 13 known subspecies of the North American cougar. Only 30 to 50 of the rare panthers are estimated to remain in the Everglades of southern Florida. The primary recovery efforts for the animal involve protecting and acquiring vital habitat, raising public awareness for its plight, and improving its overall population.

When the hockey team's new uniforms were created, the Panthers team made an initial $25,000 contribution to the

Preserving the habitat of the Florida panther is a main goal of Save the Panther, Inc.

National Fish and Wildlife Foundation. In return, as part of a fund-matching program, the NFWF matched the donation with another $12,500 for panther projects. The expansion team also issued an open challenge to the public and to corporate sponsors to support the Panther Saves program. Every time a goalie made a save during a home game, a donation was made to Florida panther projects. Bouris reports that, "Through all of our activities that season, we raised more than $50,000 for panther conservation." To raise additional funds, the team also produced an educational hockey video that was distributed by Blockbuster Video stores. The money from the rentals is matched with foundation funds, and the total amount is donated to panther projects.

Amos Eno, executive director of the National Fish and Wildlife Foundation, praises the effort. "For the first time, professional sports, corporate America, and a conservation organization have joined forces to bring attention to our rare and endangered species," he says.

For More Information

Write to the National Fish and Wildlife Foundation, Save the Panther, Development Department, 1120 Connecticut Avenue NW, Suite 900, Washington, DC 20036, or call (202) 857-0166.

Supporting the
Rainforest Habitat

After 15 years of watching the Brazilian rainforest disappear, Don Davis's firsthand view was enough to shock him into trying to save acre after acre of the precious ecosystem. Davis first went to Brazil in 1965 as a missionary. He spent 15 years traveling all over the Amazon region working with people in the areas of medicine, health, education, and religion. In 1980, he returned to the United States, but continued to travel back to Brazil once a year. "Each year, I was shocked by the lack of trees and disappearing jungle," Davis says. "Where there used to be trees all along various roads, now there were none. Timber harvesting had wiped them out. And where there used to be villages 150 miles deep into the jungle—now they were also gone because there was no jungle left."

Davis finally decided he would try and work with an environmental group to help stop the destruction. But he said several organizations told him a lengthy study would first be required to prove the need. "You don't have to study a tree falling down, the loss of a species or the loss of a living for people in the forest," he exclaims. "We needed action." So Davis started the Rainforest Preservation Foundation in Fort Worth, Texas. He began to buy acres of pristine Brazilian rainforest at about $25 an acre. By 1996, the foundation had helped preserve more than 8 million acres of rainforest in the hardest hit areas of the Amazon. Hundreds of schools, environmental clubs, and other organizations have become involved in the Rainforest Preservation Foundation's cause.

Don Davis stands by a fallen giant at a Brazilian saw mill.

The American school that has raised the most to date is Shackelford Junior High School in Arlington, Texas. Kathleen Verhalen's junior high classes have raised more than $6,000 to preserve the rainforest.

A trust fund was set up by the foundation to provide money to fight legal battles concerning land rights in the rainforest. In some cases, funds are used to hire people to protect the land from those who come to take trees for lumber. Additionally, the foundation helps train Brazilians to live on parcels of land that have already been destroyed by logging, mining, or slash-and-burn farming. Davis's idea for regenerating this land is to drill holes, fill them with nearby river sediment, and replant the land with native trees. The local people also learn to support themselves on the land while replenishing it. He hopes the reforesting effort will eventually be led by children from the cities and towns of the Amazon region. "I hope these kids will end up being the trainers of their generation and teach farmers how to live on the land without destroying it," Davis says. "They're our best hope."

Of the money raised by the foundation, only 5 percent is used for administrative costs. The rest of the money goes to the land-preservation effort. Brazilians are overseeing a large part of the program in the Amazon region, and the Brazilian government has been helpful in making the project a success by giving them preservation authority and by declaring them eligible to receive government grants.

PRESERVATION DEED

This is to certify that

ORCHARD MESA MIDDLE SCHOOL

has preserved __10.5__ acre(s) of land in the Brazilian rain forest.
All future responsibility for preservation, tax,
other liabilities will be the sole responsibility of
Rainforest Preservation Foundation.

This issued in grateful appreciation for your generosity in helping to
preserve oxygen, species of plants, animals, forest and
the general well being of our planet.

Rainforest Preservation Foundation
President in U.S.A.

Fundacao Para Preservacao da Floresta
President in Brasil

Issued on
February 22, 1996

RAINFOREST PRESERVATION FOUNDATION
P.O. Box 820308 • Fort Worth, Texas 76182

Printed on recycled paper

"I believe people can't live without the rainforest, and with modern machinery and technology, it could be gone in 20 years," Davis says. "The land bought by the foundation can never be sold, transferred or traded—it will always be preserved. We would like to teach the world about how precious the rainforest is and what a green treasure it holds. If we can prove forests are more valuable standing, then they won't be cut down."

Many certificates have been presented to those who have supported the Rainforest Preservation Foundation.

For More Information
Write to the Rainforest Preservation Foundation, P.O. Box 820308, Fort Worth, Texas 76182, or call (800) 460-RAIN.

Candy Promotes Conservation

Anyone with a sweet tooth and a conscience could help Mother Nature with EnvirOmints—you could eat chocolate and help save animals from extinction at the same time. From May 1990 to 1996, the EnvirOmintal Candy Company sold chocolate mints and donated 50 percent of its profits to non-profit organizations that work to save endangered animals and their habitats. "We wanted to get away from just sending out an envelope asking for money, like most nonprofits do," said co-founder Patrick Clarke-Delehanty. "This way people get candy instead. And it's not just another candy—the product has a tremendous educational value."

Included with each peppermint-flavored chocolate square was an animal species card. Each card featured a photo of an endangered animal, along with the date the animal was placed on the Endangered Species List and the historic range it once occupied. Additionally, customers could request a free Wildlife Action Guide from the company. The guide told people how they could take action by writing their political representatives or regional fish-and-wildlife offices. It also listed several organizations currently working to save the environment. "We provided people with educational materials to help keep them informed," Clarke-Delehanty said. "We hope it got them thinking about wildlife, and endangered wildlife in particular."

The mints were sold in about 15,000 stores around the country. "Most people say they want to do something about the environment, but they don't always have a vehicle for doing it easily and at a price they can afford," said Clarke-Delehanty. "This product gave consumers a very inexpensive and fun way to help, and learn about, endangered wildlife."

What Is Biodiversity?

Biodiversity is short for biological diversity. The term represents the belief that all organisms on Earth exist in a complex and interconnected web of life. Biodiversity stresses the need for preserving the various species of the world—or at least allowing them to evolve on their own—instead of letting humans drive them into extinction due to unnatural causes.

Biodiversity relies on preserving enough wildlife habitat for all creatures in the wild. If a habitat is healthy and abundant, the plants, wildlife, and organisms that live there will also thrive in a natural balance.

The growing populations around the world, however, are putting stress on the natural resources of the earth. More and more people are taking land away from the many animals that share the earth with us. Each year, more and more people become aware of our invasion upon wildlife habitat.

Unfortunately, many lives around the world are dependent on lifestyles that have caused species to become endangered. It's difficult to convince people to give up their jobs and lives for a few owls or a few tigers. But if all creatures exist to create a delicate balance of life on Earth, what will happen to us when many of them are gone?

In addition to the role animals play in ecosystems, plants are equally important. Plant life is a source of oxygen. Many plants also offer valuable sources of medicines. Since the majority of the world's plant species are found in the rapidly diminishing rainforests, and since most of these plants have yet to be analyzed for medicinal potential, who knows what potential medicines have already been lost due to deforestation and the loss of rare plant species.

Wildlife Management Techniques

Wildlife management is an important element in the overall conservation of species. Under ideal conditions, wildlife management can prevent human activity from threatening the existence of most species. Unfortunately, wildlife management is not operating under ideal conditions around the world, or even across America. In some places, it is a very low priority, while in other places it is completely ignored. Since many species migrate from one country to another during the year, they may be protected in one country, but not in another. In many cases, effective wildlife management threatens the incomes of people who rely on hunting, trapping, poaching, and smuggling. Some of these people have even attacked wildlife managers for interfering with their livelihoods. Fortunately, new laws and cooperative efforts around the world are helping wildlife managers do their job.

Survival School for Elephants

On the Indonesian island of Sumatra, a revolutionary and creative program aims to save the local elephants. This program teaches the country's growing human population how to peacefully co-exist with the endangered Sumatran elephants and it teaches the elephants the same lesson! When pressed for space, these elephants are known to come out of the jungle fighting mad, destroying crops and homes and even killing their human neighbors. And an elephant never forgets an enemy. "In recent years, at least 40 people have been killed by elephants in the Lampung Province," says Mr. Panjaitan, director of the forestry department of the Lampung Province. "Most deaths involved women and children who couldn't run fast enough to avoid the elephants."

Since the Sumatran elephant is an endangered species, the villagers face prosecution if they harm the rare animals. But in these turf battles for life and death, elephants have been killed. The elephant training center at Way Kambas National Park teaches both human and beast how to live in harmony. Started in 1982, the center has trained more than 160 elephants for herd management, in which trained elephants are returned to their natural domain to control the wild herds and keep them away from conflicts with civilization. This training has saved both elephant and human lives.

Sometimes a wild herd of elephants will simply enter a farmer's field or a villager's garden for easy grazing. The small-scale farmers, who are struggling for their own survival, have tried torches, electric fences, and even explosions to keep the hungry animals away, but the elephants learn to tolerate

47

A trainer at Way Kambas National Park guides an elephant out of a pool of water.

these measures. For instance, they just knock trees down to break the electric fences. Therefore, the most effective way to manage a herd of wild elephants is to return a trained elephant to the herd. Usually, these trained elephants will keep the herd away from villages, but if they approach a home or village, the people have been taught to issue commands to the trained animal to take the entire herd away from the potentially deadly conflict.

The training center began with the help of two trained elephants from Thailand. The Thai elephants were brought in to help capture the first Sumatran elephants. The elephants from Thailand lured the wild ones close enough to tranquilize them. Once sedated, the Sumatran elephants were loaded into a truck and brought to the Way Kambas Training Center. "We only capture elephants between 3 and 20 years old," says Mr. Rusman, a veterinarian at the center. The trainers can tell the approximate age of the elephant by its size.

A trainer gives a young elephant a bath.

"At this age, the animals are ideal for training. Since these animals live to be about 60 years old, the trained ones can be utilized for 40 to 50 years."

Once an elephant is brought back to the training center, it receives individualized attention. "We have one trainer for every animal," explains Panjaitan. "We typically have between 50 and 100 elephants in training at one time." Initially, an elephant undergoes a taming phase that lasts about one month. During this high-stress period, one foot is chained to a tree and human interaction begins immediately. In addition, all food is withheld for a few days to teach the elephant that meals now come from its human partners. Trained elephants are quickly introduced to the wild ones. The trained animals help calm the wild ones and impose a sense of discipline on the new animals. "When the wild elephant does something wrong, the trained one will slap it with its trunk," Panjaitan explains.

A Way Kambas elephant delivers a stick to its trainer.

While some of this training may seem harsh, the bottom line is that a few trained elephants can help to keep a lot more wild elephants alive in the long run.

After the elephants complete their first month of training, they must learn to respond to human commands. The trainers start by issuing verbal and visual commands to the giant students in combination with physical touch. At first, the elephants don't respond to human voices, but the trainers talk to their students anyway. Before long, the beasts will respond to just a simple signal and will nod their heads to signify that they understand the command. The elephants begin the day with a morning exercise program to help build their strength, because when elephants fail to get enough movement and exercise, they are more vulnerable to sickness. After their daily workout, each animal is led into a huge pond of water for a swim, a scrubbing from its trainer, and a drink of water. The individualized training sessions begin every afternoon and one of the elephant's first lessons is to raise their trunks high in the air on command. After the next few lessons, the elephants will kneel, walk forward or backward, and stop on command. The elephants will even learn to reach down with their trunks and pick specific items off the ground, then deliver them to trainers riding on their backs.

It takes approximately six months to effectively train an elephant at Way Kambas. In addition, it costs Indonesia's department of forestry about $3,300 to graduate an animal from the school. This includes capturing, vaccinating, feeding, and training each animal. Since an adult elephant eats roughly 400 pounds of food per day, a lot of time and money is spent just satisfying their appetites. The animals eat food such as corn, palm and coconut leaves, sugar cane, rice husks, and hay.

Other elephant training centers have been established elsewhere around the world, but Way Kambas is the first training center to return trained animals to the wild in order to control herds. Since they have learned how to do this, the Way Kambas team now exchanges new information with other elephant training centers in Thailand, India, and Sri Lanka to help make the training in those countries more effective. Because the training program at Way Kambas has proven so successful, the government of Indonesia has started two other elephant training centers on Sumatra. A fourth center is also planned.

Elephants are not the only graduates of Way Kambas—many villagers have also gone to the school to learn how to manage the wild animals. More than 100 villagers from Sumatra and 5 from the neighboring country of Malaysia have

Villagers near Way Kambas take part in a training program.

learned the skills of elephant control. Like the elephants, the human students spend about six months in training. "The villagers spend one month in the classroom and five months out on the grounds with the experienced elephant trainers," Panjaitan says.

The educational program at Way Kambas has boosted elephant populations in the Lampung Province. In 1982, when the training center started, there were fewer than 500 elephants in the area. In 1996, between 700 and 800 of these endangered animals roamed free in the Lampung Province. The wild population is growing so rapidly that some of the elephants are now being trained for use in agriculture and logging to keep the wild population from growing at an unsustainable rate. Although on the surface, this domestic use of elephants may not seem appropriate, it strengthens the bond between the struggling villagers and the animals that compete with them for food. The net result is a more harmonious co-existence and fewer deaths of both people and elephants.

In addition to the work being done at Way Kambas for the protection of elephants, the training center has become active in the community. Way Kambas is working with the Forum of Young People in Lampung—a social service group that helps find job training for troubled teens in the area. Through this partnership, teenagers are offered a chance to work at the training center and learn to be elephant trainers. The elephant training center has made a difference in the lives of many people. In addition to the jobs created directly at the center, more jobs are being created through tourism as visitors from around the world travel to visit this fascinating facility.

For More Information

Write to the Department Kehutanan (Department of Forestry) Gedung Pusat Kehutanan, Jalan Gatot Subroto, Senayan, Jakarta Pusat, Indonesia 10270. (They will have someone that can read English.)

Animal Detectives

Poaching has long been a practice that has taken the lives of thousands of animals around the world. However, one laboratory has decided to try and make wildlife poaching an endangered career. The National Fish and Wildlife Forensics Lab, established in 1989 in Ashland, Oregon, helps international wildlife agents build evidence against poachers and traders of illegal animal parts. "The crime lab makes wildlife investigators more effective," says Ken Goddard, director and founder of the lab, and former police investigator. "We handle wildlife crimes just like the police handle a homicide scene."

One of the lab's first accomplishments involved the 1989 international ban on African elephant ivory. Elephant ivory labeled as "mammoth tusks" began showing up at ports around the world from people's trips to Siberia and northern Alaska. Since Ice Age mammoth ivory is legal to trade, it became vital to distinguish it from modern elephant ivory. The Oregon lab found the answer to the problem in the grain of the ivory. Investigators discovered that the angle at which the grain lines cross each other is wider in elephant ivory.

However, the trade of illegal animal parts around the world is still a multi-billion dollar industry, and it is only surpassed by the illegal trade of drugs and weapons. Pelts, skins, horns, teeth, paws, and feathers of different animals make up the evidence of these crimes. Fingerprints, bullets, traces of poisons, and DNA information are all used to investigate the crimes and to try to track down the poachers. "Without a forensics lab [dedicated to the problem], parts and products from animals

This is a collec-
tion of illegal
wildlife goods
confiscated by
the U.S. Fish and
Wildlife Center.

were impossible to identify," Goddard explains. In the past, wildlife investigators have had to depend on busy university and police labs, and legal cases were lost due to delays.

Another of the lab's important accomplishments involves bear poaching. Since many Asian societies believe that bear gallbladders have medicinal value, poachers were killing roughly 3,000 American bears a year and exporting the gallbladders. The National Fish and Wildlife Forensics Lab was able to develop a method to identify the gallbladders and stop these exports. Poachers, for instance, have even been found using scientific tracking equipment to locate and kill bears that were radio-collared by scientists for biological studies. These poachers locate the radio signal while the bears are hibernating and then kill them in their dens.

The lab also helped convict a man of killing a deer inside a wildlife preserve. Genetic analysis linked the kill-site to the carcass in the man's possession. In another case, elk proteins were identified on a bloodstained knife to help convict a man of killing an elk out of season. The lab can even determine if game meat came from a male or female, which often determines if the animal was killed legally or not.

The wildlife forensics lab is the first of its kind in the world. Its 32 employees include zoologists, chemists, molecular biologists, criminalists, and forensic specialists. Projects have involved 15 different countries so far. "Most people are at a loss when they need to differentiate protected from unprotected species— especially if the material has been crafted into a usable product," Goddard notes. "If we can distinguish between illegal and legal goods, we can track down the criminals and stop the origins of the illegal trade."

For More Information

Write to the National Fish and Wildlife Forensics Laboratory, 1490 East Main Street, Ashland, OR 97520.

Rescue Center for Animals

RCAS (a Spanish acronym for the Wildlife Rescue and Conservation Association) is an orgainzation that was formed to help endangered species and promote conservation in Guatemala. ARCAS receives wild animals confiscated from smugglers and rehabilitates and releases them at its Rescue Center in the Petén region in northern Guatemala. It also works to discourage the trafficking of endangered species by educating local schoolchildren about the environmental problems associated with such illegal activities. The children, in turn, educate their parents about the problems. "We're trying our best to rescue these endangered animals and return them to their homes in the jungle," says ARCAS's director, Myriam Monterroso.

The group has taken care of 250 rescued animals since it was formed in 1989. In 1996, about 80 animals were being rehabilitated at its Rescue and Rehabilitation Center, including birds such as parrots and macaws, and monkeys, and anteaters. There was even a jaguar that was taken from a poacher when it was only eight weeks old. The animals often arrive at the center with diseases or injuries and need lengthy stays before they can be released in the wild. Animals unable to be released are offered to zoos or are bred, with their offspring released in the wild.

The Columbus Zoo in Ohio has been a big supporter of ARCAS since 1989. Through its Project COPE, the Columbus Zoo has donated more than $13,000 to the effort, along with plenty of veterinary and educational supplies, as well as hands-on technical assistance. The Columbus Zoo also promotes wildlife and rainforest conservation efforts through educational programs in Peten schools.

Beth Armstrong, leader of Project COPE, comments, "The philosophy behind this approach is that zoos have a responsibility to get involved in projects like this and be involved on a hands-on basis instead of just sending checks to huge organizations. We feel we're a part of something that can really have an impact in Guatemala." ARCAS' first reintroduction of rehabilitated animals involved the release of 36 blue-and-white-crowned parrots near the famous Mayan ruins of Tikal 30 miles from the Rescue Center.

A leatherback baby turtle heads for the ocean after being born in an ARCAS hatchery.

In addition to the work it does with animals that have been confiscated, ARCAS also has a project dedicated to preserving the sea turtle population that arrives on Guatemalan coasts to nest. The beaches of the Hawaii reserve—a protected area in Hawaii, Guatemala—are a favorite nesting ground for olive ridley and leatherback turtles. However, the eggs of these turtles are taken both to sell and to eat by the local population, and the number of turtle nests is declining every year. To help solve this problem, ARCAS has set up a program for egg collectors to donate a dozen eggs per nest that would be reburied and incubated in protected hatcheries. Once the baby turtles hatched, they would be released into the sea. Thanks to ARCAS, close to 25,000 turtles were released between 1992 and 1996!

For More Information

Write to ARCAS at their international mailing address, Section 717, P.O. Box 52-7270, Miami, FL 33152-7270, or call/fax in Guatemala (502) 2-535329. Or write to the Columbus Zoo, P.O. Box 400, Powell, Ohio, or call (614) 645-3426.

The Career of a Lifetime

The Center for Wildlife Law at the University of New Mexico was founded in 1990 by Ruth Musgrave. A lawyer, Musgrave has devoted her entire career and expertise to helping wild animals. The center is the only one of its kind in the nation and serves as a clearinghouse for information on laws governing the conservation, use, and abuse of wildlife. It is a resource for lawmakers, government officials, public-interest groups, and other people who make decisions on wildlife conservation and management.

"State wildlife laws across the country are inconsistent, which makes them very difficult to enforce," says Musgrave. "But the center has created a forum to promote better coordination among states on policies and legislation." Musgrave's first major project at the new center was developing the *State Wildlife Laws Handbook*, which summarizes and compares wildlife laws in all 50 states. The state handbook has been so successful that the U.S. Fish and Wildlife Service recently gave the center a $345,000 grant to prepare a federal version. But finding the money that is needed to support the center hasn't always been easy.

In a gamble to bring the center to life, Musgrave sacrificed her career as a lawyer—and a comfortable salary. For 15 months, she tried to raise money by writing several different grant proposals, but she received one rejection letter after another. During a period when it was getting difficult to continue the project, her mother died and Musgrave almost gave up on the project. However, while away at her mother's funeral, the funds started arriving. "When I returned home, there were no less than 15 messages from the Geraldine Dodge

Foundation," she said. "They had been trying to contact me to give the center a $40,000 grant."

The center has received more than $1 million in grant money and Ruth Musgrave's plans are far-reaching. "Our goal is to reach a point where we can actually draft legislation, mediate disputes, and teach courses for non-lawyers," she said.

The Center for Wildlife Law also organized Wild Friends, an educational project where senior citizens team up with students for field trips to the Albuquerque Natural History Museum, the local zoo, and the state legislature. The center has a "how-to" manual for other organizations that might want to replicate this program. In her spare time, Musgrave serves on the board of directors of four other organizations, including the Dian Fossey Gorilla Fund. She also teaches a class on wildlife law at the University of New Mexico Law School.

Ruth Musgrave explains to schoolchildren involved with Wild Friends what the extinction of a species means.

For More Information

Write to the Center for Wildlife Law, Institute for Public Law, University of New Mexico School of Law, 1117 Stanford NE, Albuquerque, NM 87131, or call (505) 277-5006.

These are just a few of the great success stories about wildlife management and conservation. With a little research, you can find other exciting examples around the world and possibly in your hometown. As these stories demonstrate, people can learn a lot about the preservation of our planet by understanding the balance of life that exists among animals, people, and plants. We hope that this book will inspire you to continue learning as much as possible.

Glossary

band The act of identifying an animal with a plastic or metal collar or tag with the intent of studying it.

biodiversity The combined diversity of plant and animal species on Earth.

biologist A person who studies plant or animal species.

black market The illegal sale or purchase of items.

census A detailed estimate of the population of a species.

criminologist A person involved with the scientific study of crimes.

deforestation The practice of cutting forests down in an unsustainable way; to lose forest area.

ecosystem A community and its environment functioning as an ecological unit in nature.

endangered species A species that is in immediate danger of extinction.

extinction When the last living example of a species dies.

food chain The order in which organisms feed on one another in an ecosystem.

forensic Applying scientific knowledge to legal problems.

gestation The period from conception to birth, or the length of pregnancy by an animal.

habitat The place where a plant or animal naturally lives and grows.

hydrology The study of water dynamics and chemistry of the Earth and its atmosphere.

incubate To maintain an egg under conditions favorable to hatching.

poaching To take game or fish by illegal methods.

prey An animal taken by a predator as food.

quarantine A state of enforced isolation to prevent the spread of disease.

rainforest A tropical woodland that receives at least 100 inches of annual rainfall and is marked by lofty broad-leafed trees that form a continuous canopy high above the ground.

raptor A bird of prey.

regeneration Restored to a better state.

reintroduction To return an animal to its original habitat.

slash-and-burn farming A practice in which farmers cut and burn several acres of forest every few years to grow crops. The farmers must keep moving on because the soil only yields a few seasons of crops before it is depleted of minerals. After the farmers move on, the soil usually begins eroding because it won't sustain plant life any more.

social structure The way a group of animals from the same species is organized in terms of rights and responsibilities.

soil survey To systematically take samples of soil from an area of land and then analyze the samples for their content.

species A category of biological classification ranking immediately below the genus or subgenus.

survey pole A pole about eight feet tall with large markers painted on it to indicate the measurements from one end to the other. Used as a measuring stick for distance observations.

sustainable A practice that can be done in an unlimited manner because of the minimal impact it has on natural resources.

temperate Found within the temperate zone between the tropic of Cancer and the Arctic circle, or between the tropic of Capricorn and the Antarctic circle.

tracking Locating an animal or species by various methods.

tropical From the tropics, an area defined by the tropic of Cancer in the Northern Hemisphere and the tropic of Capricorn in the Southern Hemisphere.

veterinarian A doctor who specializes in the treatment of animals.

wildlife reserve An area of land restricted to human use for the sake of preserving the wildlife within the area.

zoologist A scientist who studies animals.

Further Reading

Ashby, Ruth. *The Orangutan.* Morristown, NJ: Silver Burdett Press, 1994.

Banks, M. *Endangered Wildlife.* Vero Beach, FL: Rourke Corporation, 1988.

Denton, Peter. *World Wildlife Fund.* Morristown, NJ: Silver Burdett Press, 1995.

Green, Carl R. and William R. Sanford. *The Peregrine Falcon.* Morristown, NJ: Silver Burdett Press, 1986.

Maynard, Thane. *Endangered Animal Babies: Saving Species One Birth at a Time.* Danbury, CT: Franklin Watts, 1993.

Patent, Dorothy H. *The Challenge of Extinction.* Springfield, NJ: Enslow Publishers, 1991.

———. *Saving Wild Places.* Springfield, NJ: Enslow Publishers, 1993.

Penny, Malcolm. *Protecting Wildlife.* Chatham, NJ: Raintree Steck-Vaughn, 1990.

Pringle, Laurence. *Living Treasure: Saving Earth's Threatened Biodiversity.* New York: Morrow Junior Books, 1991.

Ricciuti, Edward R. *Wildlife Special Agent.* Woodbridge, CT: Blackbirch Press, 1997.

Index

Photo Credits

Cover: ©Martyn Colbeck/Oxford Scientific Films/Animals Animals; pages 8, 10, 11: World Wildlife Fund/Indonesia Program; page 13: Tom Maechtle; page 14: ©Miriam Austerman/Animals Animals; page 15: Russell Thorstrom; page 17: David Whitacre; page 19: Threatened and Endangered Species Information Institute; page 22: Mindy Zuschlag/Wild Dolphin Project; page 23: Will Engleby/Wild Dolphin Project; page 25: Balikpapan Orangutan Society; pages 26, 28, 48, 49, 50, 51: Gary Chandler/EarthNews; page 30: ©Terry Arthur; page 32: National Fish and Wildlife Foundation; page 35: Rebecca Villarreal/African Wildlife Foundation; page 37: U.S. Steel; page 38: Vulcan Materials; page 40: ©Joyce Wilson/Animals Animals; pages 42, 43: Kathleen Verhalen/Rainforest Preservation Foundation; page 54: ©John Cancalosi/Peter Arnold, Inc.; page 57: Colum Muccio/ARCAS; page 59: University of New Mexico, Center for Wildlife Law, Institute of Public Law.